How to Become an Educated Consumer of Website Design and Development Services

Robert Kopacz

Disclaimer & FTC Notice

Although the author and publisher have made every effort to ensure that the information in this book was correct at press time, the author and publisher do not assume and hereby disclaim any liability to any party for any loss, damage, or disruption caused by errors or omissions, whether such errors or omissions result from negligence, accident, or any other cause.

This book is for entertainment purposes only. The views expressed are those of the author alone, and should not be taken as expert instructions or commands. The reader is responsible for his or her own actions.

Adherence to all applicable laws and regulations, including international, federal, state and local governing professional licensing, business practices, advertising, and all other aspects of doing business in the US, Canada, or any other jurisdiction is the sole responsibility of the purchaser or reader.

Neither the author or the publisher assumes any responsibility or liability whatsoever on the purchaser or reader of these materials.

Any perceived slight of any individual or organization is purely unintentional.

I sometimes use affiliate link in the content. This means if you decide to make a purchase, I will get a sales commission. But that doesn't mean my opinion is for sale. Every affiliate link is to products that I've personally used and found useful. Please do your own research before making a purchase online.

DEDICATION

To my Mother and Father
Anna and Eugene Kopacz
For their patience, love, and support

Table of Contents

1 PREFACE

The Story of Ed

"If you can't dazzle them with brilliance, baffle them with bullshit." W.C. Fields

Not too many years back, I was doing some non-IT consulting work for a not-for-profit. They discovered a huge problem.

A large number of the organization's donors for that year were not listed in the annual report (anyone who has worked with large not-for-profits knows that this is a huge problem). It turned out that the list of donors which the membership and donations administrator (let's call her Jane) had submitted for inclusion in the annual report was incomplete.

The membership and donations administrator was confronted with the error at a meeting called for the purpose.

Her explanation? "The computer made an error."

I knew from my own experience, that this was an attempt to baffle in the spirit of W.C. Fields. I was not in a position at the time to say anything or confront this person. Her boss, the executive director, whom I will call Ed, already in his 70s and ignorant about computers, appeared to accept this explanation.

Because he didn't have the necessary information to evaluate Jane's statement, he could be easily baffled. When you are baffled, you concede the point, because you don't know how to evaluate it, and probably don't wish to admit that you don't know how to evaluate it.

I have been building websites for over five years now. It is my second career. Prior to this, I was a business consultant, advising companies on overall strategy, sales, and marketing. I now serve mostly small organizations, not far from where I live, building and maintaining websites for them. The majority of those organizations are small not-for-profits.

As I started approaching these organizations, or as they approached me, I started to see a pattern. Many of them did not know what to look for in a new website, how to speak with builders of websites, or how much it should cost. They "didn't know what they didn't know." In the spirit of W.C. Fields's quote, they could be easily baffled.

And unfortunately, when it comes to website design and development, there are some website professionals out there who were more than happy to take advantage of that bafflement.

The goal of this book is to educate you sufficiently about current-day websites so that you do not find yourself baffled when procuring a new website for your organization, the way Ed was by his membership and donations administrator.

I wrote it with a particular demographic in mind: The age 50 and up crowd, who find themselves in a position of leadership or management with a small, local-area not-for-profit, be it a charitable organization, trade association, or membership based organization devoted to a common hobby or interest.

They may be retired, or they may be still working, and helping the organization in their free time. They are of an age where they may have been accustomed to doing an organization's outreach and communications using printed documents, traditional surface mail brochures, posters, press releases and the telephone, whereas the world has moved on to the (for them) less familiar territory of email, websites, and social media.

It is meant to give these people a set of guidelines for

determining the best way of expressing what they need in their website to a prospective web developer, and to give them a set of tools to detect whether the website design and development company is trying to baffle them or not.

It will show what exactly to ask for so as to take full advantage of the technologies today, and still not get overcharged. To borrow a phrase from a popular commercial in the 70s, it is designed to make you an educated consumer of website design and development services.

I note that while it is aimed at that demographic group and that type of organization, a small business owner in need of a website can benefit from it as well. Be it profit or not-for-profit, if you or your organization needs a website, but you don't know where to start, this book will help you.

By learning to ask the right questions, you can signal to your prospective website developer that you know how his or her business works. It will result in a better website for you, at the right price, and a better relationship with your website professionals.

A Few Caveats

The vast majority of website designers and developers are honest and forthright in their pricing, and often welcome an educated consumer of their services. Having worked in the business for over five years now, I find website developers to be the most interesting and ethical individuals I've had the pleasure of working with.

Those who might be predatory in their business practices represent a minority. But they do exist and I have met enough clients who have been taken advantage of to know that it is worth educating yourself on how to do it right.

The goal here is to be educated, but not foolhardy. As I write this, the market for good website designers and developers is rather tight. There is much greater demand for people who specialize in the design and building of websites than there is supply. While you want to be educated, you need to also not be so aggressive as to drive people away from your project, because it might be hard to find somebody willing to work with you, and that isn't good either.

The idea here isn't to get your website built at way below market rates, but to get it at a right price, a good and fair price, and to be sure the developer isn't adding stuff to the website development that you really don't need, just to pad the bill.

Websites are fun and can be empowering for an organization that has never had one before. I hope you find this book to be both interesting and helpful. I hope it inspires you to go out and build your own website with a good understanding of how the process works and a feeling of confidence that you will be paying the right price for it.

You get the idea.

Ready? Here we go.

2   INTRODUCTION

Your First Website - The Story of Bill

When websites started becoming more common in the late 90s early 00s, chances are that you started thinking about a website for your organization. As part of the dialog amongst the organization's decision makers, someone stood up and said, "I know. My Uncle Bill is retired and does websites as a hobby. I'm sure he'd be happy to do our website for a small amount of money, or maybe even for free!"

So after some discussions, Uncle Bill became the organization's volunteer "web master". He organized the site's domain (the www.whatever.com), and even hosted it for you.

About a month after he agreed to do it, he delivered a link to a brand new, spanking website. Very cool, with the logo of the organization in the upper left hand corner, lots of bright colors, and a navigation menu. Everything was organized into these nice big tables with double borders, and there was even a visit counter that showed how many people had visited the site. There was even a little image that twirled around in the upper right hand corner! Animation! Cool! Your organization had entered the Internet age!

The site was announced to the public and well received. But when it came time to doing all the basics of your organization (the membership drives, the fund raisers, the events, the meetings, the publications), that work was still all done the traditional way, with telephones, regular surface mail, and standard paper documents (brochures, posters, fund raising letters).

The website was a nice addition, but sort of a novelty.

It remained something of a black box. You still weren't sure what it was, or how it even existed. All you knew is that you would send information to Uncle Bill to update the site, and after about a week, Poof! Like magic, the information would show up on the site. So life was good.

Then one day, around six or seven years after the site launched, you started to notice that the websites you regularly visited were looking - - well, different. The graphics were better. The layout made them easier to read. They looked like high quality magazines on a computer screen. Some of them added something called a blog, which listed news, announcements and other information about the organization. They started listing upcoming events on their site. The colors used on the site became more variated and subtle.

Cool! Their version of Uncle Bill really seemed on top of things!

Then you went to look at the site Uncle Bill runs for you. Not so cool.

What seemed like a miracle of the information age way back then now looked a bit outdated and stale. You look at the last event listed. It was from last year, but was still listed as a coming event. You recall that you sent new event information to Uncle Bill about a month ago, including the organization's Annual Gala, which was coming up in five weeks, but it still wasn't on the site. The listing of the Board of Trustees was also out of date.

You call Uncle Bill, who is now 85 and living in Florida. You mention the changes. "Oh yeah, sorry, forgot about that. Will get right to it!" he said and hangs up the phone.

Another week goes by. The site still doesn't change. After two more weeks with no changes, you call again. "Oh sorry! Forgot to tell you that I was scheduled for a hip replacement. I'm in rehab now. When I get out of rehab in two weeks I'll have a look at it."

In the last few months, people have been mentioning

to you that the website is out of date. You now start to cringe when you visit the site.

You realize it's time for a change. You have heard that it is now easier to have a website where you can log in yourself and add content, but you don't have any experience with those types of things. So you start looking around to get some proposals from companies and people who say they build websites.

After some research, conversations with other area organizations, and conversations with acquaintances, you come up with three proposals:

- Your neighbor's 16-year-old son who says he will build you a website for $500.

- A local area website developer who works on his own and provided you with a fairly professional looking proposal, says he will build you a website with the same features, for $5,000; and

- A company that specializes in building websites which has its main offices in your local area Big City, which has submitted three different preliminary designs of the site in a rather long proposal, and has offered to build the website for $15,000.

You call Uncle Bill and mention to him that you were thinking of trying to upgrade the website and got some proposals, and he said, "What for? Don't bother with any of that new fangled garbage! The site I built for you is perfectly fine!"

On top of all this, your friend who helps run a not-for-profit from a neighboring town just told you about a service called Squarespace that she has just tried out. It costs just $24 a month and she says it is really easy to use and looks great on her mobile phone.

So, now what?

The Increasing Need for Websites

For any organization with a set of objectives that they wish to achieve, be it a profit number or a fund raising goal for a charitable organization, a website has gone from

- Nice to have, to

- good to have, to

- gotta have, to

- must have, to

- can't do without,

in the course of just the past 20 years.

Our website owner in the story of Bill is realizing that. She is also realizing that, unlike other services, she is not sure how to evaluate the services of firms that build websites. I tell the story of Bill because I have heard variations of it countless times as I helped organizations migrate their existing, technologically outdated websites to current ones. Her dilemma is a common one. They are stuck. Budgets are tight. They do not know what is possible, or how much they should pay.

So, what exactly is possible today?

What is possible - A quick history

A quick bit of history and background.

In the Beginning

Back in the late 90s or early 00s, if you were a small organization, Bill or someone like him was your only option if you wanted to have a website. He was most likely using one of a number of tools, essentially software programs, to manage the organization's website. He would use the program to compose a page the same way one composes a document in Microsoft Word or some other word processing software program. He would edit the page on his PC, and then, when it was ready, upload the page to the organization's hosting account (more on website hosting accounts later), and the change would be made.

Back in those days, more complex website technologies which would allow you to log in, and then add and/or change content (much like you can now do on Facebook or some other social media) were available, but they were provided by specialized commercial software companies, and subject to large licensing fees.

Larger enterprises, for which the website was part of their key business strategy (like Amazon, or the New York Times), hired their own team of website developers, who would custom program the enterprise's website to provide those features.

Either way the cost of those types of systems was beyond the reach of a small organization. At the time, a site like the one Bill created was their only choice.

The Revolution

A few developments in the early 2000s changed all that. Young software developers, some of whom were still university students, started experimenting with new free programming languages to create website software programs that were similar in functions and features to those big enterprise websites. They also made two key decisions that changed the world of websites dramatically:

- They decided to "open the code" and let any programmer who wanted to, play with the program's "source code". If they wanted to they could even contribute improvements to the program (most commercial systems' "source code" at the time was considered proprietary and kept hidden); and

- They let people and organizations download and use the program for free.

This phenomenon was part of the "open source" software movement and is now taking the website world by storm. There are now over 200 software programs called "content management systems" ("CMS" for short) available for download, which you can use for free to run your website under an open source license. They are all "dynamic", meaning that you can log in and add, change, or delete information (in contrast, the type of site Uncle Bill created for our frustrated not-for-profit volunteer is now referred to as a "static" sites).

As of this writing, websites for the New Yorker, the White House, the Economist, and many of NBC/Universal's media properties, to name just a few, are now running on one of these open source CMSs. Can you think of any better endorsement than that?

For larger organizations, the savings have been obvious, but for smaller organizations, the effect has been nothing short of revolutionary. In the hands of a skilled website builder, any small organization today can have a website that has many (if not all) of the functions and features that the websites for New York Times or the Economist enjoy. They can even include some very sophisticated features like e-commerce, at a fraction of what it once cost to build.

With a website built using an open source CMS, our frustrated website owner in the Story of Bill would not now have to wait for Bill to get out of rehab to post new information. She could post it herself, or create a user account for another volunteer who, with a bit of training, can also post it himself. Adding and modifying content becomes as easy as writing and sending an email.

So, what do one of these dynamic, open source content management systems look like?

3 CONTENT MANAGEMENT SYSTEMS

Characteristics

CMSs have five chief characteristics which represent an improvement over static sites. These characteristics are important to know not just as a user of the site, but also as its buyer. Knowing them will help guide you in your conversations with website developers.

Easy to Add or Change Content

The first and most important characteristic of a CMS is that adding and modifying content on the site is now easy. With CMSs, the role of Bill the "web master" has now been relegated to making sure the software stays up to date and is running properly. From now on, you manage the content on the site directly. No waiting for Bill to get to it.

Easy to Set up the Basics

The second great and prominent feature of using a CMS to run your website is that in 90% of the cases, you can get a basic website up and running in five minutes. That's right. Not days, not hours. Five minutes.

It may not look like you want it to look. It may not have all the features that you want your site to have. But for a very simple site, where all you need is to add a few pages, and maybe run a list of news and announcements, it will let you log in, add the news, and display it.

It might be enough, but in most cases, it isn't.

Easy to add Features

The third important characteristic of a CMS is the ability to easily add features and functions. Most of the

CMSs permit developers to build and contribute open source subprograms which easily add new and sometimes sophisticated features to a website. These subprograms are also free to download and use by others. By downloading and installing these subprograms (called "plugins" or "modules" by most CMSs), you can extend the sites features to do things like:

- Provide an animated slide show of images on your site;

- restrict access to certain pages and create a "members only" section of the site;

- provide an e-commerce feature; and

- run an online auction,

to name a just a few.

Take note: It would also be possible to write custom programming to provide the same functions and features that the free plugin/module will provide. Many large organizations building a website using a CMS might employ custom programmers to provide these custom plugins/modules instead of using the free-to-download open source ones available. They do that because they want a more refined precise solution to the feature that they are adding.

But you don't need that for your organization. What the free plugin/module offers is almost always more than enough.

When you are looking to add a new function or feature for the site, your first question to your website's developer will be "Is there a plugin/module that can do that, *or do something close to it?*"

Do not let the developer convince you to write custom code for that feature.

Easy to Change the Look

The fourth important characteristic of a CMS is in the way it applies a graphic design to the site. Just so you know what I mean when I say "graphic design," when somebody looks at your site for the first time and says, "Wow! Nice site!" as a first impression, they are commenting on the graphic design of the site.

Just like a module or plugin can easily add a new feature, the system of templates which contains all of the site's graphic design (the layout, the choice of fonts and the color scheme) are contained in an easy "install and turn on" subprogram called a "theme". And just like you can turn off a feature added via a plugin or module with the click of a link on the CMS's administrative pages, you can change the look of your site with the click of a link the same way.

Why is that important for you? Because just like the CMS and its plug ins/modules, there are themes which are free to download and use for your site. After doing the five minute setup, and selecting the plugins/modules, you can search the internet for a free theme for your CMS, download it, install it and activate it as the default theme of your site. In the blink of an eye, your site goes from plain to nice.

But wait, you say. Don't I need a custom graphic design for my site?

That would be good to have, but it's not necessary. Even though you may think of the quality of your website by the way it looks, and you may take pride when somebody says, "Wow! Nice site!' when they first come across it, people visiting your site are looking first and foremost for information, not pretty graphics. So if money is tight and you want the website on a CMS, a CMS with a free theme will be cheaper and faster to implement than a site with custom designed graphics.

Your priority is not to make it look graphically spectacular, but to make sure it does not look bad, because a badly designed site distracts a visitor from the information on the site. Many of the free themes have been prepared by a professional designer, and will look pretty good. For sure, they won't look bad.

All your Content is in a Database

The fifth and last important characteristic of a CMS is that it uses a database to store all the content on the site. This is a very important feature which is easy to overlook. If you don't know what a database is, you should read more about it. But if you have ever done any banking on line, or used the address feature of your email service to keep track of your various email addresses, then you have used a database. With a static site, an old event or news item is often deleted and gone forever. With a CMS, it can stay live as archived content for years (more later on why that is a good idea).

The distinct benefit of having it stored in a database is that it gives your content a certain structure, which can allow it to be used in different ways in the future. The most obvious advantage is that if you wish to move your site to a different CMS, if the content is in an existing CMS and therefore stored in a database, you can now migrate it easily to that new system.

You don't need to know all the details about how the CMS retrieves content from the database to display it on the site. Just know that that's where the content is stored, and the CMS is the mechanism by which it is displayed.

The Takeaway

So, what have you learned so far?

- Someone may tell you that only a web professional can add the content to the site. Not true, with a CMS, you can. Easily.

- Someone may tell you that setting up the core of the CMS is hard. It isn't (They all take somewhere from five to ten minutes to set up).

- You may be looking for a particular set of features. Someone may tell you that it will take dozens of hours and custom programming to add the features you desire. It won't. If there is a plugin or module for the CMS that provides a similar but not identical function, you can simply accept what the plugin/module does and save yourself some custom programming time / money.

- Don't assume that your developer will tell you that there is a plugin or module that offers similar (but not identical) features. Always ask.

- Someone may tell you that you need a custom graphic design. You don't (you can download and use a free theme).

- Someone may tell you that the custom graphic design has to be added now, because to add it later will cost more money. It shouldn't. A website's theme is essentially "plug and play". Whether you create a custom theme now or create it later on down the road should not represent a material cost difference.

So Where's the Programmer?

You may have noticed one thing in the course of this conversation: In the list of common CMS characteristics, all I have been talking about is downloading, installing and configuring.

There is no software programming involved.

In fact, with a CMS, you can set up an entire website, and even one with some sophisticated functions and features, without writing or even knowing how to write a line of code in a particular programming language.

The existence and growing popularity of these CMSs has created a new type of web professional: "The site builder." These individuals have mastered the art of building a sophisticated website by choosing and configuring the right plugins or modules, and picking a free theme. No custom programming involved.

Site builders are increasingly being distinguished from "web developers." As that description suggests the person has a level of mastery of the programming language in which the CMS is written. Those professionals could write their own plugins/modules, or even write their own CMS from scratch (just like in the old days).

Their skills at programming are impressive. But for your purposes they are very expensive, more expensive than the services a "site builder", and unnecessary. You are not trying to be the next Amazon.com, nor are you building something like the New York times website (although you might be able to duplicate many of the features that those sites have).

Just because site builders don't know how to write code, doesn't mean that they cannot build great websites. Building sites using a CMS by installing the core software, and adding a set of plugins or modules, is easier than it has ever been, but that does not mean that it is easy. Skill is involved. But it is not as high a skill level as that of the true, full blown website developer.

The Takeaway

You don't need the services of a "web developer," in other words, someone who is skilled at custom programming. What you need is a site builder. In your discussions with a website professional, be sure to underscore that you don't want to pay for custom programming. You want a site that relies on the installation and configuration of plugins/modules for the features that you require, and accept what that solution can do for you. You'll pay less for your website, without compromising the functionality.

What a Content Management System is Not

As remarkable as these software programs are, it is

important to understand what they are not.

I was once discussing with a client the particular size of an image and how large the image should be relative to the text, and explained that I had to program the preset size into the CMS.

"But can't you just grab the corner and drag it to make it bigger?" she asked.

She thought that the CMS would work just like her desktop publishing software. Bottom line: it won't.

We have all been beneficiaries of the revolution in desktop software applications. Whether it be Microsoft Word or more sophisticated programs like Adobe's InDesign for desktop publishing, we have become so accustomed to the "point and shoot, drag and drop, WYSIWYG (What You See is What You Get)" ease of these desktop applications, that we immediately assume that our websites built on CMSs can do the same thing. Countless clients of mine have assumed this going in to a project.

So it bears emphasizing that, as much as the various open source CMS's have advanced over the years, and as many incredible things that they can now do, there are some constraints, and the skills you learned making more sophisticated newsletters, brochures or posters in Microsoft Word or even InDesign do not directly translate to the world of CMSs.

Instead of the completely flexible, drag and drop approach of the more sophisticated commercial desktop publishing packages, CMSs take a very structured, systematic approach. So the font size of the paragraph is fixed. The font selection and size for the title of the page is fixed. The size of the image? Fixed.

And there is a good reason for that. If you reinvent the look of every new page you create, by changing font sizes, colors, and image sizes, it essentially overrides the carefully thought out look a designer created for the site, which takes into account many universal rules of design that create a pleasing effect. If you proceed to override all that work of the designer, it not only creates a lot more work for you, it can make the site look really bad.

So, my advice to you is, when you finally own a website with one of these remarkable, sophisticated free open source CMSs, don't try to make it into a desktop publishing platform. Just fill out the form for creating a page, and hit save. Let the system do the work for you. Let the design for the site that you chose and perhaps even paid for do its job. That's what it was meant to do, and that is what makes it easier.

Those who build, maintain, and improve open source CMSs are looking for ways to make them more like desktop publishing systems. One day, you may be able to do that. But today is not that day.

Wait, There's More - "Websites as a Service"

So my only alternative is a CMS? Right?

Not exactly. Around the mid '00s as CMSs started to take hold and become more popular amongst smaller organizations, a number of companies emerged offering what I would call "Websites- as-a-service." You may also see them referred to as "DYI site builders."

With these services, you simply go to their website, create a user account with a password, and Voila! You have a website on their system, permitting you add and publish content. Most of these companies have a number of page templates from which to choose, much like the themes on a CMS, and some even let you upload your own custom template.

Some offer a free account. Others offer a free trial period, after which time you are obliged to pay a monthly fee (often as little as $8 per month). Most of the free services are limited in what they can do initially, but permit you to incrementally add features to your site by paying a small one time or monthly fee.

They are similar to a CMS, except with a CMS you own the hosting, the domain, and in fact all the files which make up your website. You can copy them down to your computer, have your site builder modify them, and even move them to another hosting account.

With these services, all your stuff (your text content, your images, etc.) is up on the company's server.

Instead of paying up front to build a website, and then having a truly nominal monthly operating cost, these systems essentially spread the cost of the website out over months. It's like leasing a car instead of buying it with cash.

As of today, companies such as Wix, Weebly, and Squarespace are the leading providers of "websites as a service". Two of the most popular CMSs, Wordpress and Drupal, run their own alternatives at Wordpress.com and Drupalgardens.com. Like the communities that build, maintain, and constantly improve the open source CMSs these companies are constantly working on adding new features and improvements.

So as of this writing, are they any good? Should you consider them as an alternative way of launching and maintaining your site?

Website as a Service - Is There a Catch?

The website as a service companies can appear tempting, but just realize that like with anything that sounds "too good to be true", there are some catches. A few recent stories can illustrate this.

The Story of myfamily.com

In 2014, myfamily.com, a service that allowed families to create their own space on the internet to share photos, stories, and family histories, decided to close. Myfamily.com was very much like one of these "Website as a service" companies, but offered many more sophisticated and complex features. It was a paid service from the start, and had been in operation since the late nineties, so close to twenty years.

As you can imagine, some families had perhaps hundreds of pictures, with as many as thousands of entries of news, announcements, family histories. So now that myfamily.com was ceasing operations, how would they get that data back?

The answer? myfamily.com offered the families a download of the pictures they had uploaded. That's it. No news data, no history data. No text which accompanied the pictures. No family recipes. None of that. The families were left with having to copy and paste all of those entries by hand from the myfamily.com site. Needless to say, a lot of unexpected work. People were furious, and went to social media to vent their anger. But it didn't change anything. myfamily.com offered no alternatives for their loyal customers and closed down as planned at the end of September, 2014.

The Story of logmein.com

At least myfamily.com gave their users fair warning. I once used a service called Logmein.com, which allowed you to log in to one of your remote computers and use it, just as if you were in front of it. It wasn't giving me a website, but it was a great free service, and I used it from time to time to access a desktop computer I had at a remote location. One day, I received an email saying that they were discontinuing free service. That very day. And that was it. If I wanted to continue using it, I had to now subscribe to their service for a hefty fee which I could not justify.

The Story of blip.tv

I've had clients who hosted on the free video hosting service called blip.tv. Blip.tv decided one day that several of its accounts were in violation of its terms of service and gave those people 60 days to download all their videos, after which time they would close the account. Not only did those blip.tv users have to spend time and money downloading the videos (if they didn't keep a backup of course), they now had to figure out where else to put them.

Websites as a Service - the Takeaway

Enough stories. I imagine that there are dozens of other stories out there and, as the corporate world buys and sells these companies, I expect that there will be more stories like this. While some of these services were not strictly offering free or low cost websites in the sense I am considering here, they were offering a service for hosting content or other service which abruptly ended, leaving the users scrambling for an alternative.

Websites as a Service - Any Other Catches?

Having the service discontinue operations, and perhaps abruptly, is one caveat to these "websites as a service". But there is another one.

Operating a dynamic site can be a liberating experience when you were previously stuck on a static site and dependent on a web master. At first, you are not sure what to expect, and then pleasantly surprised that you can add content yourself (maybe even gleeful). You feel delighted with your new website, its straightforward features and your newfound powers. You'll feel this at first with either a self-hosted website that runs on a CMS, or a service like Wix or Weebly.

But after a while, as you start focusing on how to create a better experience for visitors to your website, you start looking around at other websites, and see features that you sense would be good for your site. You start thinking "I wonder if I could do that with my current site?"

At that time, if you are using one of these "Website-as-a-service" companies, you are going to start experiencing some constraints. They will tell you they don't offer that particular feature and can't say whether they will in the future. Or they maybe able to add features for an additional monthly fee, and all of a sudden that "low low" price you enjoyed at the beginning isn't so low anymore.

A dynamic website is considered dynamic not just because you can easily add new content to the site. If you're doing it right, you are constantly looking at your site, looking at your site's traffic, listening to your visitors and supporters, taking suggestions on what to add to the site, and thinking about adding features.

At one point in time, based on your experience with the site, you are going to want to make some changes, or add some features. Each website is different, and it's hard to predict when this will happen, but I can almost guarantee it will happen, and when it does, you won't be happy about it.

Which Way Should You Go?

If you are a small, local historical society for a small town, and you might just run two or three events a year, and really do not have any news to speak of, but you want a web presence with a donation button and an email contact form, then many of these "Website as a service" companies might be better for you than a self-hosted CMS. Even with the caveats mentioned in the prior chapter, if you are truly on a tight budget, it is better to get started online with something that works well, rather than nothing at all.

But if you have many events, activities and news items each year, and are seeking to materially increase your donations, event attendance, or improve whichever performance indicator you use, then I would go with a CMS as a "self hosted" website. You will spend more up front, but you will get the better result you seek.

As the foregoing chapters suggest, a self-hosted site gives you far more control of your site from the very beginning. It's yours. It will give you the power to immediately address what you wish to do with the site in the future, no matter now nuanced and subtle, some of which might be hard to even anticipate right now. It is not held captive somewhere out "in the cloud," where you may or may not be able to download it in the future.

The frustrations with what you can't do with your DIY website will emerge sooner than you think. So you might as well just start with a CMS to begin with. It does require a bit more investment up front, but over the years, if you spread out the cost as a monthly figure, you will end up paying the same or perhaps just a bit more than with these "Websites as a service" companies.

If you are convinced that you want to start with one of these services, all the caveats mentioned above notwithstanding, the lesson to take away from this section is to not think so much about how to get started on one of these services. That's easy. Make sure there is a good way to end the relationship if you feel you need to. And that means at the very least having a way to get all your information out in a format that other systems can import.

Then when you are ready to consider a self-hosted CMS for your website, you can pick up this book again at this location and continue reading.

A Quick Observation - "Use it or Lose it"

So, you know now your options. You've got a few basic suggestions on how to choose between a self hosted Content Management System and signing up for a "website as a service". From this point on, I will assume that you have chosen a self-hosted Content Management System as your approach, and the advice from this chapter forward will focus on that.

Before I get into the "How" of dealing with the website professionals, I just want to take a moment to make sure that the "Why" in place.

I've heard the comment hundreds of times before. "Why pay money for a new website? Nobody visits the current one."

For me, the foregoing statement is like saying, "Why own a car? It can't take me anywhere," when you haven't bothered to learn to drive, pay for the gas, maintenance or insurance. I am assuming that because you are reading this book, you understand the benefit of having a website and seeking out a more effective one. Using one effectively to promote your organization requires an understanding and belief that the Internet is now the most effective way to market your organization (which it is), and that dominance will only increase in the future (which it will).

But to be clear: To make it effective, you have to get traffic to the site. And getting that traffic requires a certain amount of work. You just don't build it and expect people to come.

In order to get that traffic, at a minimum, you need to post new content regularly.

This assumes you have new content to post on a regular basis, and most organizations do. There are upcoming events to post - "great new event next month!" - , there are reports on recent past events - "what a great event we had last week!" - announcements of awards or acknowledgements given, honors received by the organization, grants received, and (if you are a grant-giving organization) grants awarded. New officers and/or trustees are appointed. Personal profiles of benefactors can be posted in a profile section, or profiles of trustees. There is a lot of information you can share with your visitors.

When you own a dynamic site and you wish it to be effective as a marketing and outreach tool, you are in the publishing business - whether you like it or not.

Content strategies for websites are covered in other books, and the scope is simply too large to go into detail in this one. But you must embrace the fact that managing the content on your site and getting people to read the content on the site will gradually, or even swiftly, replace the old methods you used to use.

In this book, from now on, I am going to assume that

your organization sees the benefits of a dynamic site, wants one, and is ready to change the it promotes itself. But remember that a dynamic site by itself is not the solution. It is a tool to enable more effective solutions.

4 WHAT DO YOU NEED: WHICH CONTENT MANAGEMENT SYSTEM SHOULD I CHOOSE?

So, up until now, I have described what a CMS is, why it represents an improvement over static sites, the alternatives to a CMS other than a static site, why a CMS might be better than those alternatives, and why you would want to do more than just update the site from time to time.

We will now discuss which ones you should choose from, the one I recommend, and why.

The Top Three

There are over 200 CMSs out there from which to choose.Tthe three most popular ones are Drupal, Wordpress, and Joomla! (yes, the exclamation point is part of the name. Don't ask; I don't know why. I'll probably skip it in future references). Those three have the most websites currently in operation, or as website professionals like to say, "in production," or more colorfully, "in the wild".

You should ignore all the others, and use one of the Top Three. You should also look with suspicion on any web professional who recommends anything other than the Top Three for your new website.

Why?

Once a site builder builds your site for you, that investment should last you for years, with minimal input from a "web master." You or your staff (if you have one) or other organization volunteers will be helping you do manage the content. You will to do software updates periodically, and sometimes a security release is issued which must be applied to the site's software, which your web professional should do for you.

Or you may wish to change something. Or, as remarkably reliable as these systems are, every once in a great while something breaks, and you need to contact the person who helped build the site to fix it.

But what if that web professional is not around anymore?

The more obscure the CMS is, the harder it will be to find a developer with expertise in that particular CMS. The Top Three CMSs listed above have huge and growing communities which support them. They are all on the rise. They are, in a way, competing with each other for the top spot amongst open source CMSs.

There will be a lot more website professionals in your area who are experts in one or more of the Top Three CMSs than an obscure one. You should not be the subject of some web developer's experiment with a new CMS that he ends up dropping because he didn't like it, or for which there are no other website builders within a 200 mile radius.

The Takeaway

You should ask prospective developers which content management system they are using. While I will explain my preferences amongst the Top Three in the next section, if that developer does not name one of the three CMSs mentioned above, walk away. They might explain to you the benefits, they might try to convince you of the benefits of that system.

WALK AWAY. Look for a developer who has expertise in one of the Top Three CMSs. You'll be glad you did.

So Which One of the Top Three Should You Choose?

One of my favorite sayings is "if you're a hammer, every problem looks like a nail." In the web development community, as a website builder / programmer, you will naturally gravitate toward the CMS that you personally find the most appealing, and for which you have a particular knack, or about which you know the most.

Comparative analyses of the Top Three are everywhere on the web. All you need to do is Google "Drupal vs. Wordpress vs. Joomla" (without the quotes) to come up with dozens of articles comparing the three. The bottom line for all three is that each has its pluses and minuses.

I will have to admit that I am a hammer for Drupal. I have been building sites in Drupal for over five years. I started building websites in Wordpress, because I had heard of it and it seemed that everyone was using it. Then I taught myself Drupal, and while I still help some clients with Wordpress sites, all of my new websites are built in Drupal.

So of these Top Three, for the small not-for-profit, be it a museum, local historical society, or membership based organization, I advise you to go with Drupal. But it's not just because I happen to like it, or have a knack for it. I also happen to think that it is the best one for you.

There is one very good and compelling reason I say that. Your website's technology is only as good as its ability to enable a content strategy. A well developed content strategy drives traffic to the site, and produces the benefits of more donations, better event attendance, and the like. Your website needs to be able to enable a nuanced content strategy to succeed, and to be able to quickly implement a change in strategy, if you need one.

In order to effectuate such a content strategy, you have to be able to create relationships between items of content. This is something that Drupal has been able to do for years now, and its capability to do that is only getting stronger. The other two may be working on some similar capabilities, but if they are out there or under development, I have not found them.

Drupal also permits your site builder to do something the other two cannot do easily: Create a customized administrative process for your content managers.

Website designers and builders think long and hard to make the websites you visit easy to use. The administrative pages of a website, where you go in to add or modify the content, should also be easy to use. Drupal excels in that area.

There may be other web professionals who read this and might disagree, some vehemently. I am sure people will continue to compare the Top Three and have their favorites. This competition for supremacy only helps you, the consumer of website design and development services. For my money, Drupal is the way to go, not only for what it can do for you now, but what it will be able to do for you in the future.

In the hands of a competent website programmer who specializes in that system, any of the Top Three will give you a great website, one that will be a huge improvement over Bill's static site described at the beginning of the book. So if you go with any of the Top Three, you will be already well ahead of the game. You can and should do your own research, consider what I have said here, and let your own judgment be your guide.

5 WHO DO YOU NEED - THE FOUR KEY PROFESSIONALS INVOLVED IN THE WEBSITE CREATION PROCESS

So, you've now had a recommendation for the list of CMSs you should choose from, and which one I think you should choose. But no matter which one you end up choosing, you will need some professionals with certain skills to get your site up and running.

In this new world of CMSs, who exactly builds the website? I am going to discuss who these people are, what they do, and why it is good to have that minimum skill set working for you.

The Graphic Designer

Designers, in their purest form, are responsible for the entire visual look of the site. When people go to a website and at first glance say, "Wow! Nice website!" they are in fact complimenting the site's graphic designer.

Those graphic designers may have started designing what we now refer to as "hard copy" marketing materials (as opposed to digital materials, like websites), and then added websites to their repertoire.

A custom graphic designer's fee for a website can easily run to a few thousand dollars. So, do you really need one?

Are there benefits to hiring and paying a graphic designer? Yes. If you can afford it, the fee is often well-justified. These days, the entire look and feel of the site can have a positive impact on the entire website visitor's experience.

That does not mean that you have to have a design

that is going to win awards. These days, free themes are available which will make your site look good without huge design fees.

Your goal is not to compete with the major websites of the world for the ultimate design. You just need to make sure that it just doesn't look bad, because a bad design will distract visitors from the content.

So the rule is, if you can afford a graphic designer, go with one. But if you can't afford one, a good free theme will do the trick.

The "Information Architect"

If you have a site which is beautifully designed, after browsing the site, says visitor says, "Yeah, it's a nice looking site, but I really had a hard time finding what I was looking for," then your information architecture has failed.

An information architect will think through and help you decide exactly how all the information on the site will be labeled and organized so that visitors to the site will easily find what they are looking for. It will involve deciding what goes in the main navigation menu of the site, and what does not go in there, how each page is structured, what should be in the sidebar for each page, and the like.

You may think that "hey it's simple, and thinking about this is overkill." Don't dismiss it. The way you organize the information on the site might even be more important than the site's graphic design.

You can read the real life case study below for an example of how information architecture can fail, or you can skip ahead to the next chapter. But the case study below is a perfect example of how poor information architecture can take away from your site visitor's experience.

I see examples of sites built on CMSs with poor information architecture all too often even from companies that should know better. So it is easy to get this wrong, and worth the trouble to think it through with a web professional to get this right.

Case Study – Good vs. Bad Architecture

Let me give you a great real life example of bad information architecture. Some names and circumstances have been changed to assure anonymity.

All content management systems have by default something called the "basic page". The form for creating a basic page consists of a page title and a place to add and display the body text of a page. These types of content are typically used for things like the "About Us" page.

The body text of all basic page creation forms on all systems come with a formatting toolbar, much like the one on a wordprocessor, which allow you to do a number of useful things, such as:

- Insert an image into the text area and align it left or right;

- insert a link to another website on the page;

- make text bold, italic, underscore etc.;

- align the text of a paragraph to the left or the right;

and other formatting options.

I have one historical society client that runs a website which I built for them. One of the volunteers decided that he wanted to reproduce the daily journal entries of a soldier from the Revolutionary War who was born and grew up in a nearby town.

To do that, he created a basic page like the one I have described above, and added all the information from the journal entry into that basic page's body area (which was the only place to put it on the basic page create form).

So, if today was January 15th, he would enter that soldier's January 15th journal entry from 200-plus years ago. Where possible, the member would insert images which depicted places or events referenced in the journal entry, using the toolbar features described above.

When it came time for the next journal entry, he would add all the information from the next journal entry in that same existing basic page that he originally created, by editing it and adding the next journal entry just underneath the previous entry.

It went on and on like that, journal entry after journal entry, for dozens of journal entries. In order to find a particular journal entry, you had to scroll down the page, and scroll. And scroll.

If you wanted to find a particular date, you had to either keep scrolling down the page until you found it, or use the search feature in the browser to find that specific date.

What if you would like to find all the entries where a particular public figure of the time or a particular place was mentioned? You would have no choice but to use the browser's search feature and then search for the name, and then you could only find them one entry at a time. There would be no way to see a filtered list of just those journal entries where that particular item was mentioned. Nor would there be a way to search all the entries for a particular key word, and then list all the entries with that key word in a search results page.

Do you see what's happening here? Do you get a sense of how a user can get frustrated trying to experience this page? Do you get a sense of how that feature on that historical society site could be reorganized?

Let's see how a website developer with a good sense of information architecture might go about reorganizing how this feature is "architected" to make for a better experience, both for the site visitor and for the content manager.

First, because the feature involves potentially dozens of new items of content, a new custom content type could have been created, Called "Journal Entries". It could have had a special date field which used the date calculation features that most of these sites have to store the actual date of the journal entry. This could permit sorting lists of the entries by date order. Those lists could have been simply teasers, which a visitor could click through to read the desired journal entry. The list could have had perhaps ten to fifteen journal entry teasers per page, with a pager at the bottom to avoid the endless scroll.

There could have been a special field for a featured image, which depicted the subject matter of the entry. There would, of course, be a body text area, the same as the basic page, for all the text of the journal entry itself.

Finally, a field could have been added to this custom content type to allow for "free tagging". "Tagging" is a type of taxonomy, a way to organize large quantities of content by subject matter. Free tagging has the advantage of allowing you to apply an existing tag, or if one does not exist, to automatically create the tag when you type it followed by a comma. You could then add as many new tags as you wanted, followed by a comma (For example, typing "Valley Forge, Morristown," without the quotes in this field, would either apply the tags "Valley Forge" and "Morristown", or create them if they did not exist).

You could then, in the sidebar, create a list of tags, which the visitor could scan and click on. That list would be automatically updated to include all new tags added. Clicking on one tag would take you to a listing of just the journal entries tagged with, say "Washington."

Once a few entries have been created, those entries can now all be organized in a variety of ways. You could have a very short list of just the dates. Click on the date and it takes you to the journal entry for that date. Or you could have a list of so called "teasers" described above, which provide the entry date, the featured image, and the first 100 words of the entry, followed by a "Read more" link which takes you to the full entry.

Do you see the difference? The point here is not to come up with the perfect way to organize this data, just to show you that by thinking about it in a more structured way, to consider the architecture of the information, will give you the opportunity to give the visitor to the site who finds that feature interesting a realm of choices on how to read it. That's what thinking through the architecture of a feature can do for you.

Building a feature like this onto an existing site wouldn't take an experienced website builder more than three or four hours, but the benefits to the website owner in terms of a better visitor experience when viewing the feature would be profound.

Sub-specialty - the User Experience ("UX") Expert

There is a sub-specialty to information architecture. It's called user experience, or UX for short. You want a good user experience for your site, not a bad one.

You can say that that is the end game for any site owner. If a visitor to the site can't find what they are looking for or can't figure out what the labels for all the links in the navigation mean, then your site doesn't really serve its purpose.

There are user experience specialists out there. They will make suggestions on where to put things on the site and how to label them. They will often test sites by putting someone in front of a computer, opening your site in a browser, asking them to find something, and then noting down what happens.

Web professionals are constantly pondering the relationship between graphic design, information architecture, and user experience. When reading about these disciplines you will see lots of discussion and graphics with intersecting circles. You can say that the outcome of good graphic design and good information architecture is good user experience. That doesn't necessarily mean that having gone through the exercise of information architecture and graphic design on your site will provide a good user experience. But the only way you will know is by having someone who doesn't know your organization go to the website and try to find something.

You do not necessarily need a UX expert on board on your site, but you should be aware that a good user experience is what you are aiming for.

The "Developer"

In the purest sense of the term, the website "developer" is the person charged with taking what the information architect has created and building all the mechanisms and displays necessary to add, modify, and display that information to a site visitor. The developer assures that all those features for adding custom content are in place and working properly.

As I discussed in the Chapters on CMSs, thanks to these new open source CMSs, the old days of hiring a software programmer to custom code your site are gone. The main job of the website "developer" is to find all the right modules or plugins, add them to the site, and configure them. If he or she must write some custom code, it is only after careful consideration and rejection of an applicable plugin or module, and only then if it makes sense cost-wise to do so.

This phenomenon has led to the creation of a new web professional, the "site builder," someone who knows how to build a website without writing any code. So, while I am labeling this role as one of "developer," I am really, in your case, speaking of a site builder. The difference is that all developers can build or code, but a builder can only build and not code. For a small site, that's OK. It will save you money. These days, you can have some remarkably sophisticated features on even a small site, without having to write code from scratch. Using a site builder will operate as a constraint on possible features.

We are using the term "developer" here because many people are familiar with it, and also because many a site builder will also use it, even if they do not know how to code. But a site builder is what you are looking for.

Be wary of the ego factor here. Many a site builder may feel insecure about not knowing how to code. They may think that you are asking this question because you are looking for someone who knows how to code. You may wish to reassure them that you are looking for a competent site builder, and not a custom coder.

The "Themer"

In between the developer/site builder and the graphic designer there is someone known as a "themer". Lately, if he or she has more advanced programming skills, he might have the sexier title of "front end developer."

A themer is required only if there is a custom graphic design commissioned for the site.

This person knows the HTML programming language and CSS, the programming language used to apply the designer's design to the website itself, or more specifically to the website's theme. This task is known as "theming." Depending on the site and the technology he or she uses, it can be the most time demanding part of the site's development, and is probably the most important, after the designer's role, in determining whether people will say, "Wow! Nice site!" when they see your site for the first time.

Normally, the themer will get the site after the designer is finished, and after the site builder is finished building.

Pulling it all Together

Your team does not need to be a group of innovators. They only need to pull together a website that does not look bad and makes it easy for a visitor to navigate.

Ideally four different individuals, each with one of the

titles described above ("Designer," "Information Architect," "Developer/Site Builder," and "Themer") would be on that team. However, retaining and paying four different individuals, be they employees who are part of the same company or individually retained, can get expensive.

The good news is that all these skills can be found less than four people.

You will often find a site builder who can also theme, and who also might have experience with information architecture. The designer might also know HTML and CSS, and may therefore know how to theme a site as well.

Can the graphic designer and the developer be one person? That's rarer. I'd even go so far to say that an award winning graphic designer and an award winning site builder cannot exist in the same person. However, there are website developers /site builders like myself who know something about design. They may not win any awards for their designs, but their sites don't look bad.

As a rule of thumb, the more one person can do, the fewer individuals, the less expensive the site will be to build.

The Takeaway

When you are talking to freelance site builders or web agencies, and they propose four different people, one for each discipline, ask them if for example, the site builder also knows something about site architecture, and if you could save any money by skipping the information architecture specialist.

If they have a graphic designer that they wish to pull in, and the estimate for design is large, ask about using a free theme for the site for the time being. The very fact that you know a free theme is available might cause the design estimate to go down.

As a rule of thumb, individual freelancers will be more

likely to be "Jacks of all trades" when it comes to the four core skills. So, if you are on a tight budget, you may wish to look for a local freelancer rather than go to a web agency for your professional services.

6 WHAT DO YOU ASK FOR - HOW TO WRITE A REQUEST FOR PROPOSALS

Overview

Now that you know something about the technology, and something about the disciplines required, it's time to start understanding how to solicit proposals.

Larger organizations, both pubic and private, when looking for quotes for any large project, often prepare something called a request for proposals, or RFP for short. Sometimes they refer to it as a request for quotes ("RFQ"). In this book, I will use RFP.

If you want to get a good site at a good price, you should write one as well. It will take some work, but it will be well worth it.

Writing an RFP that shows that you are an educated consumer of website design and development services will do several important things.

It will signal to all firms out there that you are such an educated consumer. It will also make it easier for them to provide a quote. Finally, a well written RFP will permit you to more easily compare proposals from competing website professionals.

Signaling your savvy to them might also cause them, perhaps even unconsciously, to be more judicious with the number that they provide. Finally, it will help govern the relationship with the website developer during the course of your website's development.

I've got seven secrets to writing a great RFP for a website. They are listed below. I am listing them, more or less, by order of importance, with the first secret being the most important.

Secret 1 - Think Through the Dynamics of the Organization

When preparing your RFP, it is a good time to think about what your organization currently does, and what you would like to have it do.

Do you run many events, or just one a year? Are you trying to increase attendance? Would you like to do more events in the future than you are doing now?

Are you looking for money donations? In-kind donations, such as a contribution to an existing museum-type collection of items? Do you wish to increase those donations?

Do you have a collection hidden away that you would like to have online, so visitors can browse through it?

The website will become the single most effective tool for communicating with current supporters, gaining new ones and growing your organization. Think about not just where your organization is now, but where it's going, or where you would like it to go. It will go a long way to help you define your website needs. Write it all down, in collaboration with those who manage and steer your organization. Share it with to your prospective web professional. It will go a long way toward getting a truly effective website.

Secret 2 - Speak in Terms of Features

The dynamics of your organization will help tell you what features you need on the site.

The term "features" is something of a term of art in the web design and development world, and if you break down your site in terms of the features, it not only makes the site easier for the website designer/builder to price, it will also make the cost more realistic.

Recall our chapter about what a content management

system is, and what it is not. CMSs serve you best when you think of your content in structured terms. Organizing the RFP in terms of the features you desire is honoring this approach.

When you break your site's structure into features, you take a systematic approach. So organizing it into content types, like News, Events, Programs, and Publications, helps the web developer enormously when it comes to pricing your site.

The first place to look for features for the new site is your current site (if you have one). What were you using it for? Were upcoming events posted there? Reports on the outcome of past events? Official meeting notices? The classic "about us" page?

The next group contains types of content you would like to post on your new site, but haven't because it was too complicated to maintain on the old static site. For example, a feature listing and providing information about the Famous Houses in a historic community might have been just too much to keep up effectively.

If you don't have a website, then the work product analysis in Secret 1 will be your key guide.

Static ("Evergreen") vs. Current ("Short Shelf Life")

There are essentially two types of content for every website. Static content, which doesn't change very often, and current content (think "current events" from school), which becomes old more quickly.

Things like the "History of our Organization", or "About the Society" aren't going to change once they are posted. It is the type of information that you might have in your print brochures. This type of content is sometimes referred to as "evergreen content".

Then there is content which has a short shelf life. An upcoming event falls into this category. So will the list of officers. Their shelf lives might be different, but they change more frequently than a page called "The History of Our Town" will change.

In contrast, with short shelf life items like news or events, the content will grow stale after a short time. An upcoming event, after a few weeks or a month, will become a past event. News, after a month might become old news. At the end of a term, a president will become a past president.

You should first categorize your content as to whether it is static or a current. You will probably find that you have much more content that can be easily classified as "current".

Single Page displays and Lists of Stuff

For most features of this type, you might wish to have the full details of each upcoming event displayed on a single page. You would also like a page which displays lists of the same content, such as an easily scannable list of all upcoming events.

Thinking through all these things in detail will help whoever is building your site provide a more accurate estimate of the cost. If you do just one thing in preparation of the request for proposals, do this.

I'll give you an example of what a feature description might look like when I provide sample RFP text later on.

Secret 3 - Speak in Terms of User Stories

If you put user stories into your RFP, the jaws of those site builders who review your RFP will go slack.

User stories are part of a software development management technique used by teams of web developers working on larger sites. The technique, just so you know, is called SCRUM; and it is an "Agile" approach to website development.

"Agile web development" is an approach to project management for websites which favors the approach of launching a website quickly with the minimum features, and then add new features frequently to constantly improve it. Think of building a house which has all the basics first, and then adding additions as you need them. The nature of software development makes it easier to do that with a website than with a house.

As part of the SCRUM method, the web developers conceptualize new site features in terms of user stories to help guide them in building the features. You will note that with a website, there are a minimum of two potential users: The person who visits the site to get information, and the person who adds the content to the site.

How Might a Typical User Story Look

Lets say that the site has a need to list events. Without the concept of a user story, one might simply write something like this:

"The Society would like to list events on its site."

The user story for the events feature might look something like this:

For the anonymous visitor to the site:

"When I arrive at the home page, I would like to see a listing of the next event or events that the organization is having somewhere on the page. I would like there to be a page of all the events as well, so that I can easily scan the list and see what types of events are coming up, and to see if there are any I would like to attend. After scanning the list of events, I would like to have the option of clicking on one of the events to view the full description. I would like to know where the event is taking place, the price of admission, and perhaps a link to take me to Google Maps so that I could click and see where the event is, exactly. If I want to go, I would like the option of generating directions on Google Maps so I can see how to get there."

For a site administrator:

"In order to add an event, I would like to simply open a

form on the site after logging in, add the name of the event, the date, and the location, and a brief description of the event which would be optional. I would also like to add an image to the event listing, which would also be optional. Once I hit save, I would like the event to be immediately published, and also automatically go to the listing of events, in ascending date order. To get the location to show up on a map, I would like to be able to simply include the address of the venue and have the site automatically find the location on a Google map and display it. I would like to be able to change the number of events listed on the front page to add more or fewer events, as needs be. I would like all event listings to be automatically updated so that when the next coming event date passes, it will come off the list and the next event in line will appear at the top."

In the second one, you are being very specific. You are even giving the web developer a lead on the overall site's architecture. This will give the developer a better idea of how to price your site.

You can and should write a user story for every conceivable feature, and at a minimum, you should have two user stories for each feature: The visitor to the site, and the content administrator.

You can easily find your user stories by examining your frustrations with your current website. Obviously it is not doing something you wish it could do, otherwise you wouldn't be shopping for a new website. Turning your list of frustrations around into an ideal into a Dream wish list is part of developing the user story. The more user stories you can think of for each desired feature to make part of your RFP, the better.

Secret 4 - Create a "Need to Have" and a "Like to Have" List

Recall what I mentioned about SCRUM in Secret 3 on User Stories? Part of the SCRUM / Agile philosophy (I'm paraphrasing and taking some liberties here) is to launch quickly and add new features often. You can apply this philosophy to your site as well.

So, when you are preparing your RFP and you are on a tight budget, decide what you simply must have at a minimum at this stage. It might suffice right now to just have an about us page, together with a donation button, and how to volunteer, a "news stream", and an events listing. Save the photo galleries, the feature about the town's most important homes, and the like for later. Ask in your RFP for a price for your "need to have" features and your "like to have features." This will give you more options when analyzing price estimates.

Secret 5 - Migrate the Content Yourself

You may think that building the site is the hardest part of the project. Or maybe the graphic design?

Neither of those things. The single most difficult thing to do is to create the content for the site (if you don't already have one), or migrate the existing site content to the new site (if you have a static site).

If you have been using your old static site to archive lots of historical content, then content migration could become both cumbersome and costly.

I will not go into the details of what factors go into the migration of content from a static site to the new dynamic site, because each situation is different, except to say that in your RFP, it is a critical factor to consider when you are on a tight budget.

So, ask the developer to break out the price of content migration as a separate quote. If it's too much and breaks your budget, you can always get volunteers and staff to enter the content to the new site. While that might take longer, it will be cheaper and also double as a training exercise.

For some sites, this might be a big job, but if it helps get getting you the site you desire within the budget you have, it will be worth it.

Secret 6 - Ask for Video Tutorials

Content management training is a constant issue with a new dynamic website for small not-for-profit organizations. Many of those involved with the organization are volunteers, who are not involved with the organization every day. They might be involved with the website even less. Under those circumstances, it can be easy to forget how to manage content on the site.

To solve this problem, in the RFP as part of the scope of the project, ask for a series of of video tutorials on how to use the site. These are easy to do (there are a number of free open source "screen casting" software programs to choose from). They can be easily added to the website itself, with the content restricted so that only content managers with log in privileges on the site can watch them. This will save you hours of "back and forth" and potential extra support fees after the site is launched.

Remember: When evaluating an estimate for this specific feature: An hour's worth of video tutorials only takes a bit more than an hour's worth of time to record, let's say 70 to 80 minutes. A dozen video tutorials anywhere from six to nine minutes in length (which is more than enough) might take just over two hours to record. Building the feature into the site, with the necessary restricted access, should require no more than a few hours of a site builder's time. Don't let anybody tell you that it's going to take more time than that.

Secret 7 - Get a Separate Quote to Make the Site "Responsive"

"Responsive Web Design" is the name for an innovation in web technology that makes having a custom optimized view of your site on mobile devices easier.

Note: I said "easier," not "easy."

You might be thinking, "Nah, we don't need that." Two years ago, I might have agreed. But things have changed since then.

Once your site is launched, you can expect that not less than 30% of all visits to the site will come from some sort of mobile device, either a smart phone or a tablet. That number will increase in the coming years. Some sites are already getting 50% or more of their visits from a mobile device.

If your site is not responsive, visitors will have to tap and pinch the screen with their thumb and forefinger to read the content of your site. They will have to scroll the site around back and forth to see everything.

With responsive design, everything will be clear and easily readable on a mobile device.

So in your proposal, you should ask for responsive web design quoted as an option, and with a separate price. This will not only get you a price estimate, it will signal to the prospective site builder that you know what responsive web design is by asking for it.

7 PULLING IT ALL TOGETHER - THE RFP

Here's a sample RFP for a historical society using the principles just described.

The Anytown Historical Society - Description

You represent a historical society in a town (pop. 20,000) in the Northeast. Your town has a rich history going back to colonial times. You hold in your collection a number of historical artifacts from the town, and also have a number of books for sale which chronicle the town's history. You have information on many of the historic buildings in town, and information on the more prominent families who had an influence on its development.

You put on about ten events per year, most of them in the Summer in conjunction with the library. You would love to do more, as you find this stimulates cash donations and interest in local history in general.

You are also promoting an ongoing archaeological dig on the grounds of one colonial area residence where there was once a forge. So you are continuously seeking funding for the on-site digs and investigations, mostly in the form of grants.

Naturally, you are always seeking funds in the form of donations from local residents, and people who would volunteer in the administration of the Society. You would also like to get some more general grants to cover operating costs, or for projects which might come up in the future.

You currently do not have a website, but would like one as you feel the time has come. So you have received a grant of $10,000 for, amongst other things, helping to build a website for the Society. You do not need to spend all the grant monies on the website. Anything you do not use can be used for general purposes.

Proposal - General Considerations

"We are interested in a website built on the Drupal open source content management system. We are interested in the following set of features, to deliver content to satisfy the following user stories. We wish to avoid custom programming for the features set forth, and wish to use contributed modules to provide these features. Where some modules provide some but not all of the features desired, please set this forth in your proposal explaining how the contributed module falls short or differs from the desired feature. We will reserve the right to modify the feature requested to conform to the module."

COMMENTS: I of course have recommended Drupal in this case, because I generally recommend Drupal, but in fact you could substitute Wordpress if you like or Joomla. Emphasize that you do not want custom programming, and will conform your needs to whatever the plugin or module gives you. My only strong recommendation is that you make it one of these Top Three.

Proposal - Content

Site Features

COMMENT: Writing User Stories and a list of Features is something of an iterative process. You may write up a list of features, and then start writing your user stories, and through that process uncover a few more features, which you can then add to the list.

"The Society expects to have the following features on the website.

- Events

- News

- Photo galleries

- Board member listings

- The historic forge as a separate feature, with its own landing page, description, events, and news galleries

- A place to list publications for sale

- A place to subscribe to a newsletter

- A donation button where people can donate money online

- Social media buttons so that visitors can both share items of content on social media and also follow the Society on social media.

User Stories for the Society Site

COMMENTS: Provide your user stories here. What would your user stories look like? I provide examples below for just a few to help you get started. It might seem like a lot of work, but going through this exercise will help you save money on the website.

User Stories

When they Visit the Front Page or Home page

As a visitor to the front page of the site I would, first and foremost like to get a general overview of what the historical society is about, the name of the town and the state in which it is located, in a brief statement (200 to 300 words) on the front page. I would like regions on the front page that list the most recent news and the upcoming events. I would like to see a "callout" or "teaser" to a special landing page for the forge. I would also like to be invited to a "Donate" page which will explain the benefits of donating to this Society.

Events

As a visitor to the site, I will be able to learn of all

upcoming events on the site. When the user clicks on one of the next upcoming events, the user will go to a page which displays a the date and location prominently on the page, together with the name of the event and a full description. A link on the page will allow the visitor to get directions from Google maps. The event page will also display a list of links related to the event, both from outside the the site and to relevant pages within the site. For example, an event concerning the forge might link to the landing page for the forge on the Society site. It might also link to articles or pages on other websites, such as the presenter's website.

When reading an event on a single page, the other upcoming events should be available in the sidebar so that the visitor does not have to go to the home page again.

When I click on the link to the page called "Events", it will lead to an easily scannable list, with teasers of the events appearing, say five to a page, and a pager at the bottom permitting me to page through the list for upcoming events. In all lists of events, the next upcoming event would be at the top of the list, with the following events listed in ascending order. On this page, they might only see the name of the event, the date, and the location with a "READ MORE" link to get the full description.

News

As a visitor to the site, I will be able to easily read individual news articles on the site in much the same way as I would an Event. I will be able to find the most recent four or five news items posted to the site, on a block, in a region of the front page, with a link at the bottom of the block that takes me to a page that lists all news headlines. All news will be listed in descending order, with the most recent news item posted at the top of every list.

I will be able to click on the headline of one of the most recent news items to go right to that item and read it. On that page, I should be able to scan other recent news items in the sidebar so that I can also see what other most recent news items are there to read, without going back to the home page of the site.

There will also be a page on the site which provides an easily scannable list of news, with a pager on the bottom, so that I can page back through the list to see what news items are there. I should also be able to browse the list by category.

The Forge

As a visitor to the site, I would like to be able to go to one page and read all the information about the historic forge. I would like to read about its history, have easy access to most recent news items about the forge posted on the site, and also learn about upcoming events related to the forge. I would also love to have aggregated in one place all news about the Forge from other news sources on other websites.

Prominent Families in Town

As a visitor, I would like to be able to read the history of each of the families in town, by first going to a single page that has a list of all the families. From that list, I can choose to read about one family by clicking on the family name. Once there, I can see a family tree for that family. I should be able to read the biographies of family members who were prominent. As with the forge, if there is information about the families on other websites, I would like to have a list of links of related websites where I can read more about them.

What is Your Need to Have/Like to Have List?

COMMENTS: In this section, having done an exhaustive list of features, you are now doing triage. You are explaining to the web professional what you consider essential, what is optional from the above list, and you are asking the estimates for what you consider optional features at this time be itemized.

"We would like to have the following features broken

out and the price itemized as optional features. It should be clearly stated whether the itemized options are in addition to or included in the total site price.

- A landing page for the town's prominent families

- Prominent Historical Buildings of the Town

- Select items from Society collection

- A place to put videos of the events."

Video Tutorials

The Society would like to have a set of video tutorials available to content managers on the site, restricted only to those who have content administration rights on the site, so that they can go back and reference them in case they forget how to do something. The videos should also be suitable for new content administrators. Please state this as a separate item with a separate price.

Design

Please provide a separate itemized quote for the site's graphic design. The Society reserves the right to use a free theme for the site at this time.

Content Migration

COMMENTS: This site does not have an existing site. In this case, one of two things could happen: 1) let the web developer add it, or 2) you add it yourself. The second alternative saves money and acts as a training exercise.

"The Society volunteers will add the content to the site themselves, after the training videos are added to the development version of the site".

8 SO, HOW MUCH SHOULD IT COST?

So, the $64,000 question: How much should all this cost?

As you can imagine, developers are reluctant to toss numbers out there, because "each site is different", and in fairness, they have a point. Having said that, the organizations I am addressing, be it a small historical society, membership-based group, or museum, have many of the same needs and characteristics, so I think it is easy to find a range.

One group (you should subscribe to their newsletter and read their blog) called Networking for Good, posted a presentation on their site from 1999, in PDF form, addressing exactly this issue..

The presentation addressed the needs of not-for-profits specifically and has a lot of good information on how much websites should cost, and much of what they report there, albeit in abbreviated format, I have found to be accurate. A few points to consider when evaluating a price:

It takes a minimum of 20 hours of professional site builder time to simply build the site. As a professional service provider, I have found it hard to do it for less than that;

Site builders currently (2015) charge anywhere from $75 to $125 per hour for their services, with $100 being the average.. Either they will quote you that hourly rate, or provide you with a lump sum amount that was calculated based on a rate in that range;

That would put the fee for just building a really simple site in the $1,500 to $2,500 range; and

Most customized website designs cost at least $1,500 and can go up from there. You should budget anywhere from $1,500 to $3,000 for the site's design.

Responsive web design is a special case. You will note that the PDF I linked to does not mention Responsive web design, because it essentially did not exist in 2009 (smart mobile devices did not appear on the market until late 2007 with the introduction of Apple's iPhone).

Responsive design is part theming, part building, and part design. It affects all three of the key disciplines of building a site. The designer has to come up with a look for each "view port"; the themer has to apply the design for each separate view port to the site, and the developer or site builder might have some configuration issues to deal with on the site. I would count on anywhere from $1,000 to $2,000 to budget for responsive web design.

What does this pull together? A site that has:

- News;

- Events;

- Listings of officers and directors;

- Photo galleries;

- Pages for the organization's history and the about us page;

- A page soliciting volunteers and donations;

- Contact forms; and

- A special feature content type to list the historical houses of the town (as an example of specialized custom content); and

- Which has a custom design and is responsive

would probably cost somewhere between $5,500 and $6,000 without the responsive feature, and $7,000 to

$7,500 with the responsive feature.

If you take out the design costs (using a free theme instead), the cost would probably fall in the $3,000 to $3,500 range.

As a general rule of thumb, the more features you have on the site, the more expensive it will be.

These numbers do not include the cost of content migration, which can vary too widely from site to site. But these guidelines should give you some sense of what it should take, and whether you should let the site builder handle the content migration or do it yourself.

9 THE DEVELOPMENT PROCESS

All website developers have their own way of building a site and reporting to the client during the development process. What I am explaining here is one general way to do it. It is not the only way, and your developer might even have his or her own way of doing it. But most development processes follow something like what I am about to describe.

If you are Designing – Wire Frames and Comps

If you choose to hire a graphic designer to design your site as part of the process, you will need to go through that exercise with the designer.

Each designer has a different way of going about that process.

Does your organization have an existing logo or branding scheme? If so, then that should be your starting point. The color scheme and style inherent in the logo will be your designer's clues as to how the site should look. The designer may wish to look at other "branding materials where your logo appears, such as newsletters, brochures, letterhead, and the like. If you have those types of marketing materials, the site should look consistent with them.

If it does not have a branding scheme, or if your logo feels outdated to you and you can afford it, ask the designer to design a logo for your organization. It will probably require a bit more money, but might improve the results of the site if you do it.

If you are starting from a clean slate (no website, no existing marketing materials), or even an archaic website, the designer might ask you to point to three or four sites you like and ask why you like them. This is an important part of the design process.

There are also tools out there to build something called a "mood board". These were often done manually, in physical form, and comprised of photos, graphics, and perhaps quotes, headlines and articles that captured the mood that you wished to capture with the site. There are now on line tools that permit you to create and share a mood board on line. You might not encounter it in dealings with your designer, but in case you do, you will now know what they are.

After that, the designer might put together something called a "wire frame", followed by something called a "comp".

A wire frame provides a rough layout for the site, showing what features would go where on all of the key page templates. The designer, perhaps working in conjunction with the developer/site builder, following known principles of site layout based on research and experience, might suggest various layouts that will optimize the site visitor's user experience.

A "comp" which is short for "comprehensive", is a mock up of the actual site design, often done in Photoshop or some other illustration program, following the layout rules set forth in the wire frame. It will include the logo, all the various fonts selected for the site, and the color scheme with perhaps some real images from your collection of images inserted just to give it better context in reference to your organization. It should come very close to what your actual website will look like.

NOTE: My experience has been that no matter what you do,the final website will always look a tiny bit different from the comp. This is normal and should be anticipated. I am not sure what causes this but it happens in all the websites I build.

A "Draft" Site on a Staging Server

While the site is being designed, but after the wire frame has been created, the developer/site builder might already be working on adding the various features to your site and making sure that the layout is already in place. Once that is done and the design has been approved, either the site's builder or a separate person engaged to "theme" the site will get to work.

Remember, the themer is the professional who takes what the designer has designed and applied it to a special templating system called a theme which serves to display the site in a browser.

The site builder is doing the work on a local development environment, which is a feature on the site builder's computer that makes it work just like a website server. This lets the site builder work faster, since everything is right there on the computer. When it is ready for presentation, your inspection, or approval, it might be transferred to a "staging" server or sometimes a remote development server. This means that your freshly built website will be on a temporary URL so that you can access it easily via the web.

When it is approved, it will then be moved to your domain on your hosting account.

10   OWNING A SITE

Once your site is built and launched, there are a few things to remember when operating it.

Acquiring and Maintaining Shared Hosting

Your new website has to have a place to live. The neighborhood where it lives is called a website server, and the lot on which it will be located   in that neighborhood is called a hosting account, or is sometimes referred to a "shared" hosting account (since you share the website server with your neighbors, the other hosting accounts on the server).

The site also has to have a name, which is your site's domain name. All domain names are essentially leased, and not owned. The process is called "registration." Domains can usually be registered with the same hosting company from which you purchase shared hosting, but it does not have to be with that hosting company. It can be registered elsewhere. Permit the registration to lapse and someone else can register it, and then it isn't yours any more.

Most modern CMSs run best on Linux operating systems. Linux, for those who have not heard of it, is a free open source operating system for computers, which was started by a Finnish programmer called Linus Torvalds (it also shares a lot in common with the Unix operating system for computers. Hence the name Linux). Linux is now the preferred operating system for most website servers, for the simple reason that it is faster and more efficient, and there are no licensing fees, so it is cheaper.

As of this writing, a good quality shared hosting account, which would be perfect for a small organization, be it for profit or not-for-profit, using Linux costs around $80 per year. To buy it, you need to go to the hosting company's website with a credit card, and be prepared to create an account on the site with user name and a password.

If you already have a hosting account for your static site, you might not be able to use it for your new dynamic, CMS- based site. Most of the static sites used by smaller organizations usually had someone build their sites using a software program called FrontPage, a Microsoft product that provided a word processor-like interface for creating static website pages. Since FrontPage was a Microsoft product, most who opted for a website created in FrontPage also acquired a shared hosting account based on Microsoft website hosting technology.

Unfortunately, the open source CMSs I am discussing, while they can be made to run on Microsoft web hosting technology, do not run as well, and (I'm just guessing right now), most site builders don't even support building a website on Microsoft technology.

So, be prepared to check what type of hosting technology you are currently using and if it is Microsoft, be prepared to switch. You'll save money with the switch long term.

A Couple of Tips on Purchasing Hosting

Make sure that the hosting company offers "shell access". Shell access is a way to work on the server using the command line. Those of you who remember computers before Microsoft Windows came around and having had to start software programs from the "command prompt" back in the '80s already know what shell access looks like. If you are wondering, in this wonderful age of graphic desktops on computers, why having a command line would be an advantage, the fact is that the nice looking desktop and those menus and buttons add a lot of operating overhead to a computer's performance. They in effect slow it down. Many tasks can that can be performed from that graphical desktop can be performed faster from the command line.

Check to see if the hosting package offers version control. Those hosting accounts which offer shell access might also have version control. Version control is a nifty technology that your developer will love to know is there. As with shell access, this might not be listed as a feature, but it could be available as a silent feature. The hosting company's support line should be able to tell you.

If you don't have a website yet, purchase the hosting before you get the domain. Many hosting companies will offer you one year domain registration free when you buy the hosting first.

Don't buy hosting for several years in advance. Just buy it one year at a time. Most hosting companies will try to hook you into a multi year purchase, and offer material discounts for such a long term purchase. Resist that sales pitch. Many of these companies are being bought and sold by larger hosting companies. The marketplace is shifting all the time, and a company which was once considered high quality could change when the board in a corporate acquisition makes a strategic decision to cut back on quality to save on costs. Today's high quality shared hosting company can become tomorrow's poor performer in a very short time. You protect yourself from this phenomenon by purchasing just one year in advance.

Don't buy anything else. When you start the process of purchasing hosting, many companies will try to upgrade the sale by selling you a ton of other stuff along the way. None of it is necessary. The only thing you should consider purchasing in this process is the privacy protection for your domain (if you are acquiring the domain at the same time).

Should I Host With My Developer?

Many web shops have their own servers and offer hosting. Should you host with them? In my opinion, no you shouldn't.

There are of course advantages to having your website's developer host the site. They have probably spent a lot of time configuring their server so that it runs perfectly for the type of CMS you are hosting. If the website's developer will also be looking after the site and monitoring it for software security updates, he will probably perform updates on it. When it is on his server, that will be a bit easier for him to do.

The downside is that if your website's developer is a sole operator, and he or she gets hit by a bus tomorrow, you might have a hard time getting access to your site.

Maintaining ownership of of the hosting account gives you much more control over your website. You know where it is. You are the one paying the provider directly. And should you choose to change website developers, you can do so much more efficiently.

Even if you do host with your website professional, be sure to keep the domain registration under your control. I've seen organizations choose to let their website professional register the domain. Then the web shop went out of business and it became impossible for the organization to recover its domain in a convenient way.

There is no material incremental advantage to having your website professional or "web shop" maintain the registration. Renewals of domain registrations are cheap and can be put on automatic renewal with a credit card. So save yourself a potential future hassle and do it that way.

Add New Content on a Regular Schedule

Adding new content on a regular schedule will generate benefits in a number of ways.

The volunteers in charge of updating the site will become well trained in how the site works.

Regularly adding content stimulates the search engines like Google to index your site. The more they do that, the more likely you are to appear in search engines for any given search.

A big part of the increase in traffic to the site, and consequent improvement in organizational performance of the organization will be because people are finding the site through a search conducted in a search engine. So, the more likely you are to appear in search engines, the better.

"This Content is Old, So I Should Delete it, Right?" Wrong!

I have had several clients who were new to a dynamic website, and approached "updating" the website the way they would in updating a hard copy newsletter: Open last month's news letter, delete all the old content, and insert the new content.

It's a perfectly logical approach, based on how you used to do things. It is also wrong.

Whenever you delete a page on the website, a visitor who has the URL from that page, whether it is from a search engine result or because it is in their browser's bookmarks, saved that particular page for a reason. They were looking for something in that particular page. If the page is deleted, when they click on their link they will get a "Page not Found" error message (sometimes referred to as a 404 error amongst site builder types).

The collective wisdom of website ownership and usage as a marketing tool dictates that you want to provide your site visitor with 100% satisfaction. That visitor, not having heard of your organization, has come up with a page on your website somehow, and saved that link or clicked on it for a specific reason. If they click on it and get a "Page not found" error, you create a small amount of negative goodwill.

So don't unpublish or delete content if you don't have to.

Software Updates

All of these content management systems are subject to monitoring for operating bugs and security issues. Be sure to ask your website professional to monitor the site for you, perform all updates when they are required, and be sure that he or she does a backup of the site after doing each one. Be prepared to pay for this service.

I have encountered many sites that never bothered to maintain the software on their sites. They either started to break, or they were hacked, or sometimes both.

A website with a security vulnerability is a dangerous thing. It can not only affect your data on the site, but it can adversely affect anonymous visitors to the site. The cost of maintaining the site is nominal. Think of it as fire insurance on your house. It is unlikely that the house will burn down, but you still don't forgo fire insurance on the house. You should apply the same principle to assure that all updates to your CMS are applied when they are released, be they bug fixes or security releases.

Maintain a Small Reserve for New Features

Whenever I start doing the layout and design for a new website, and the client has never used a CMS before, I tell them that whatever their budget is, they should save a portion of it for making modifications to the site three to six months after launch.

Any new website is really just a hypothetical. It's hard to know what you really need at the beginning. After you start using the site, you will realize that some things need to be tweaked, maybe some features added that you hadn't thought of.

These are things that emerge in the course of using the site, and only in the course of using the site. They are hard to anticipate in advance. The reserve to make corrections will help you relieve those constraints when they occur.

11   CONCLUDING THOUGHTS

The sophisticated website of the type I have been describing here is the future of marketing for organizations big and small, public and private, as more traditional promotional channels quickly become a think of the past. For your organization, having an effective online presence has never been more important. Creating the right one for your organization has also never been more bewildering.

I hope this guide has given you a good set of guidelines to go out and speak with someone like myself with confidence and an understanding of the process.

12   FOR FURTHER INFORMATION

Together with the publication of this book, I will be writing a blog on the subject of websites for small not-for-profits. You will be able to find it starting in February, 2015 at my website, http://kopacz.biz Feel free to visit, subscribe to my newsletter to stay up to date.

13   THANK YOU!

Thanks very much for purchasing this book. If you liked it, I would appreciate your help. Please take a moment to write a review of this book on Amazon.com. I read all comments and take them into consideration when writing future editions of this book, as well as other books in the future that will help you navigate in this new world of digital marketing